The Story of Civil Rights

By Wil Mara

Project Editor Allison Singer
Editor Radhika Haswani
Senior Art Editor Ann Cannings
Art Editor Kanika Kalra
US Senior Editor Shannon Beatty
Editorial Assistants Namita Gupta, Amina Youssef
Jacket Coordinator Francesca Young
Jacket Designers Dheeraj Arora, Amy Keast
DTP Designers Ashok Kumar, Dheeraj Singh, Jagtar Singh
Picture Researcher Deepak Negi
Producer, Pre-Production Rob Dunn
Producer Niamh Tierney
Managing Editors Laura Gilbert, Monica Saigal
Managing Art Editor Diane Peyton Jones
Deputy Managing Art Editor Ivy Sengupta
Art Director Martin Wilson
Publisher Sarah Larter
Publishing Director Sophie Mitchell

Educational Consultant Linda Gambrell
Subject Consultant Kyair Butts

First American Edition, 2018
Published in the United States by DK Publishing
345 Hudson Street, New York, New York 10014

A catalog record for this book is available from the Library of Congress.

ISBN: 978-1-4654-6927-4 (Paperback)
ISBN: 978-1-4654-6928-1 (Hardcover)

DK books are available at special discounts when purchased in bulk for sales promotions,
premiums, fund-raising, or educational use. For details, contact:
DK Publishing Special Markets,
345 Hudson Street, New York, New York 10014
SpecialSales@dk.com

Printed and bound in China.

The publisher would like to thank the following for their kind permission to reproduce their photographs:
(Key: a-above; b-below/bottom; c-center; f-far; l-left; r-right; t-top)

1 Getty Images: Bettmann. **3 iStockphoto.com**: diane39 (br). **5 iStockphoto.com**: bonniej. **6–7 iStockphoto.com**: duncan1890. **8 Getty Images**: FPG (crb). **Library of Congress, Washington, D.C.**: Harvey B Lindsley, LC-USZ62-7816 (cla). **9 Alamy Stock Photo**: Everett Collection Historical (br). **10 Library of Congress, Washington, D.C.**: Anthony Berger, LC-DIG-ppmsca-19305 (tl). **11 Alamy Stock Photo**: Photo Art Collection (PAC). **13 Alamy Stock Photo**: Everett Collection Inc. **14 iStockphoto.com**: kickstand. **15 Getty Images**: Bettmann (crb); Thomas D. Mcavoy (bl). **Library of Congress, Washington, D.C.**: Frances Benjamin Johnston, LC-USZ62-40527 (tl); Frances Benjamin Johnston, LC-USZ62-78481 (ca). **17 Alamy Stock Photo**: IanDagnall Computing. **19 Getty Images**: Bettmann. **20–21 Getty Images**: Underwood Archives. **21 Library of Congress, Washington, D.C.**: LC-DIG-ppmsca-47375 (crb). **22–23 Getty Images**: Don Cravens. **24 Getty Images**: Bettmann. **25 Alamy Stock Photo**: SiliconValleyStock / Mario Chiodo, renowned human rights sculptor, www.FreedomMarchOfArt.com (cb). **Rex Shutterstock**: AP (cra). **27 Getty Images**: Michael Ochs Archives. **29 Getty Images**: Bettmann. **31 Getty Images**: Burt Shavitz. **32 Getty Images**: Michael Ochs Archives. **33 Rex Shutterstock**: Granger (cr). **35 Getty Images**: Bettmann. **36 Getty Images**: Flip Schulke Archives. **39 Getty Images**: National Archives / Newsmakers. **40–41 Getty Images**: Frank Scherschel / The LIFE Picture Collection. **42 Rex Shutterstock**: F&A Archive (clb). **43 Alamy Stock Photo**: Everett Collection Inc. **45 Getty Images**: Hulton Archive. **46–47 Getty Images**: Buyenlarge. **49 Alamy Stock Photo**: Jim West. **50 Getty Images**: Paul Liebhardt (tc). **51 Getty Images**: Historical / Corbis Historical. **53 Getty Images**: Daniel Leal-Olivas. **54 Dreamstime.com**: Laurence Agron (cla). **Getty Images**: Mark Reinstein (crb). **55 Alamy Stock Photo**: White House Photo. **56 Alamy Stock Photo**: Frances Roberts (c). **57 Dreamstime.com**: Monkey Business Images (tr); Wavebreakmedia Ltd (cl). **Getty Images**: NurPhoto (br)

Cover images: *Front*: **Alamy Stock Photo**: Everett Collection Historical cb, GL Archive cl, National Geographic Creative (Background); **Getty Images**: Robert Parent cr; *Back*: **Getty Images**: Francis Miller / The LIFE Picture Collection ca

Endpaper images: *Front*: **Alamy Stock Photo**: Newscom; *Back*: **Alamy Stock Photo**: Newscom

All other images © Dorling Kindersley
For further information see: www.dkimages.com

A WORLD OF IDEAS:
SEE ALL THERE IS TO KNOW

www.dk.com

Contents

4   Chapter 1: What are civil rights?

14   *"Separate but equal"*

16   Chapter 2: Taking action

24   *Ruby Bridges*

26   Chapter 3: Marching for equality

36   *"I have a dream"*

38   Chapter 4: Time for change

46   *New laws*

48   Chapter 5: The fight goes on

56   *How to be an activist*

58   Quiz

60   Glossary

62   Index

Chapter 1
What are civil rights?

Civil rights are laws that a government makes to protect its people. These laws make sure people are treated fairly and with respect.

One of the best parts of living in a free country is having civil rights. Your civil rights keep you safe from harm by any person or group. Your civil rights protect you so that you can live your life without fear.

The only time a person may lose their civil rights is if they break the law. Imagine how hard it would be to live without civil rights!

Education is an important civil right. Without it, not all children would be allowed to go to school.

Many slaves were forced to work on big cotton, tobacco, and corn plantations in the American South.

Not everyone has always had their civil rights in the United States. African-Americans struggled to gain civil rights for many years.

In the early 1600s, thousands of people were taken from their homes in Africa and sent to North America on ships. Once there, they were sold as slaves.

A slave is someone who is owned by another person. Slaves were used as workers. Many of them worked on large farms called plantations.

Slaves worked long hours. The work was very hard. Slaves were treated like property instead of people, but they could do nothing about it. They had no civil rights to protect them.

There were people in America who wanted to stop slavery. They were called abolitionists (ab-oh-LI-shun-ists). Some

abolitionists, such as Harriet Tubman, helped people to escape slavery in the South. They traveled to the northern states and Canada by a special route known as the Underground Railroad.

Harriet Tubman

Tubman, who was a slave herself until she escaped in 1849, guided hundreds of slaves to freedom in this way.

Frederick Douglass was another famous abolitionist. As a slave, he learned to read in secret.

Frederick Douglass

When he escaped to Massachusetts in 1838, Douglass began using his talents as a writer and speaker to convince people that slavery was wrong. He wrote his first book in 1845. In it, he tells the story of his life. This book has now been read by people all around the world.

Booker T. Washington was also born a slave. He went on to become a great writer and public speaker. Washington believed that African-Americans should be allowed to have an education. In 1881, he founded the Tuskegee Institute, a black college, in Alabama.

Booker T. Washington speaking to African-American students in 1912.

Abraham Lincoln

Abraham Lincoln was elected president in 1860. He was an abolitionist. He wanted to end slavery in the United States once and for all.

However, other people wanted slavery in the United States to continue. They were not happy that Lincoln was elected. Many of these people lived in the southern United States, where farming was a big part of their lives.

A war between the southern states and the northern states began soon after Lincoln became president. This is known as the Civil War. More than 600,000 people would die before the Civil War finally ended.

The Civil War was fought from 1861 to 1865.

The northern states won the Civil War in 1865, and Lincoln passed a new law. This new law ended all slavery in the United States. It is known as the 13th Amendment to the Constitution.

Even though they were no longer slaves, African-Americans were still treated unfairly.

They usually found it difficult to get jobs. Sometimes they were not able to buy homes, or to eat in restaurants and buy things in stores that only allowed white customers.

If a white person attacked a black person, the white person almost never got in trouble for it. Sometimes the black person would go to jail, even if he or she had done nothing wrong.

African-Americans were still a long way from having their true civil rights in the United States.

Black people were often separated from white people at public places, events, and gatherings.

"Separate but equal"

Some states had laws called "Jim Crow" laws that allowed segregation. To segregate means to separate. White lawmakers wanted black people to live separately from white people. They often used the phrase "separate but equal," but things were rarely equal—not even close.

There were separate public bathrooms, water fountains, and other facilities for white people and black people.

Late 1800s

Schools for white children were in the nicest buildings. They had new textbooks and well-trained teachers. The schools for black children were often not as good.

1940s–1950s

Years later, schools were still segregated in the United States. Students were still not being treated equally or fairly. Something had to be done.

Chapter 2
Taking action

African-Americans still were not being treated equally at the end of the 1800s. For example, there were sometimes separate train cars for black people and for white people.

In 1892, a black man from Louisiana named Homer Plessy refused to leave a train car meant for white people only. He was arrested, and found guilty. Plessy and his lawyers believed he had not done anything wrong. They brought his case all the way to the United States Supreme Court.

Plessy lost again. The Supreme Court's decision told the rest of the country that segregation, or treating people as "separate but equal," was fine.

However, there were signs of hope. In 1905, about 30 African-American leaders got together to talk about the challenges they faced. This historic meeting led to the creation of the National Association of the Advancement of Colored People, or NAACP, in 1909.

In 1940, this North Carolina bus station had separate waiting rooms for black people and white people.

COLORED
AITING ROOM

IVATE PROPERTY
NO PARKING
through or Turning Around

COACH COMPANY
45

In 1954, the "separate but equal" way of thinking started to come to an end. Places that were meant for African-Americans, such as schools and restaurants, were not equal to those for whites. Lawyers for the NAACP started lawsuits to allow African-American students to go to the same schools as whites. This time, the Supreme Court agreed with them.

Unfortunately, many schools still tried to keep out African-American students. In 1957, nine black teenagers in Little Rock, Arkansas, weren't allowed to go to Little Rock Central High School.

The president at the time, Dwight D. Eisenhower, had to get involved. He ordered the school to let the students in.

Elizabeth Eckford, one of the nine students, bravely ignored protests as she walked to school in Little Rock, Arkansas.

After that, the Civil Rights Movement became stronger and stronger in the United States. This is when another major African-American figure in the movement showed up— an Alabama housekeeper and seamstress named Rosa Parks.

Rosa Parks was fingerprinted after her arrest for refusing to give up her bus seat to a white passenger.

In December 1955, Parks was sitting on a bus in the town of Montgomery, Alabama. The bus was filled with passengers. When a white man got on, she was told to give him her seat.

Tired of this unfair treatment, Parks refused. She was arrested. She also lost her job as a seamstress. Little did the town of Montgomery realize what an awful mistake it had made.

Rosa Parks in 1992

After Rosa Parks's arrest, leaders in the African-American community were angry. It was time to take action.

They organized the Montgomery Bus Boycott. A boycott is when people refuse to use the services of a business in the hope of convincing the business to change its behavior.

This photograph shows Rosa Parks, first in line, boarding a bus after the Montgomery Bus Boycott ended.

African-Americans in the Montgomery area were encouraged to boycott public buses. The boycott lasted more than a year, from December 5, 1955, four days after Parks's arrest, until December 20, 1956.

Finally, the state's top court made a decision. The bus company's segregation rules were declared illegal.

Ruby Bridges

In 1960, when she was just six years old, Ruby Bridges took an important test. She did well enough on the test that she was allowed to attend William Frantz Elementary School—but the school had always been for white students only.

From Ruby's first day, she was treated terribly. Other parents refused to let their children go to school with her. Most teachers refused to teach her. But Ruby was brave.

Ruby was protected by federal marshals, who walked her to school each morning. She refused to cry during her walks to and from the school.

Her family also suffered during this time. Her father was fired from his job, and some stores refused to serve her parents.

Today, Ruby stays busy with civil rights activism. She has received many awards and honors. In 2014, a statue of her was unveiled in the courtyard of the William Frantz Elementary School.

Chapter 3
Marching for equality

One of the most important figures in the Civil Rights Movement was Martin Luther King Jr. His dream of equality inspired millions of people.

King was born in Atlanta, Georgia, on January 15, 1929. His family was very poor. As a young boy growing up in the South, he was treated unfairly many times. His family was not allowed to shop in certain stores, or to go to restaurants or public places that were only for whites. From an early age, he knew this was not fair. He wanted to make things right.

King earned a college degree in religious studies. In 1954 he became the pastor of a Baptist church in Alabama.

At the church, King worked hard to improve his skills. He wrote many speeches, and proved himself to be a powerful public speaker. These talents would become very useful in the fight for civil rights.

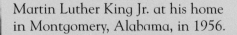

Martin Luther King Jr. at his home in Montgomery, Alabama, in 1956.

On December 1, 1955, one of the most important days in King's life took place when Rosa Parks was arrested for not giving up her seat on a bus. After King heard about this event, he helped lead the boycott against the Montgomery bus system. By the time the boycott was over in December 1956 and the buses were no longer segregated, King had become famous across the country.

King and the Montgomery Bus Boycott inspired others to take action. In 1960, four young African-American students in Greensboro, North Carolina, sat down at a lunch counter in a Woolworth department store. Because they were in a whites-only section, no one would serve them. Still, they came back day after day.

Each day the students came back, more people came with them. Soon there were more sit-ins taking place all over the country. The sit-ins were successful. Many department stores stopped allowing segregation.

African-American students taking part in the sit-in at a Woolworth department store in Greensboro, North Carolina.

Some African-American leaders took an aggressive approach to the fight for civil rights. One such leader was known as Malcolm X.

Malcolm Little was born on May 19, 1925. In the late 1940s, he changed his last name to "X." The "X" stands for his original African name, which he did not know.

Malcolm X believed that African-Americans could depend only on themselves to gain their civil rights. He did not think they could depend on government leaders.

Malcolm X encouraged black people to take action against others, even to the point of violence if necessary. Many people disagreed with his ideas about using violence.

Malcolm X speaking at a civil rights rally.

King giving a speech to a crowd on October 16, 1965, in New York City.

King disagreed with Malcolm X. He believed that violence would make some people feel even more hatred toward African-Americans and their cause.

Instead, King believed in nonviolence. He advised people to keep their protests peaceful. This included taking part in marches, sit-ins, and boycotts. He also advised giving speeches and writing books and newspaper articles.

A 1960 newspaper ad written by civil rights leaders

King often spoke of the power of love. He believed that love was the way to equality. Some people disagreed with the idea of African-American equality, but many people had respect for King.

One of the largest protests in the 1960s was a march in Washington, DC, in August 1963. About 250,000 people came! They gathered in front of the Lincoln Memorial. Leaders of the Civil Rights Movement gave inspiring speeches. King's speech had a big effect on the people at the event. The speech also inspired people around the country who read about it later.

Together, the people had asked the government for equality. They wanted new laws that would end segregation and discrimination. The march inspired government leaders to begin working on these new laws.

But that was later. There was more work to do first.

On August 28, 1963, many people came out with signs and banners to take part in the March on Washington.

"I have a dream"

Martin Luther King Jr. will always be
remembered for his famous "I have
a dream" speech. He gave it during
the March on Washington in 1963.
In the speech, he spoke of the struggles
African-Americans had faced in the past,
and the struggles they continued to face.

. . . I have a **dream** that my four little children will **one day** live in a nation where they will **not be judged** by the **color** of their skin, but by the **content** of their character. I have a **dream** today. . . .

Chapter 4
Time for change

The 1960s are thought of as the turning point for civil rights in the United States. Many people of all races took part in protests and marches to tell their government that things needed to change. They asked their elected leaders to make laws that would end racism and discrimination. They wanted African-Americans to be treated fairly.

The government listened. Two presidents helped to bring about the change people wanted to see: John F. Kennedy and Lyndon B. Johnson.

President John F. Kennedy (left)
and the vice president at the time,
Lyndon B. Johnson, in 1961.

In November 1960, the voters of the United States elected senator John F. Kennedy president. Kennedy had been raised in a wealthy family. He wanted to ease the struggles of people less fortunate than himself.

Kennedy became President of the United States on January 20, 1961.

In March 1961, he created a new law. It required all government workers and people who apply for government jobs to be treated equally—regardless of their "race, creed, color, or national origin."

In 1963, Kennedy began working on new laws that would protect all Americans from discrimination. However, Kennedy was shot and killed in Dallas, Texas, on November 22, 1963, before he could finish this work.

Kennedy's vice president, Lyndon B. Johnson, became president. He promised to make sure that all of Kennedy's plans would become reality.

The Civil Rights Act of 1964

And they did—on July 2, 1964, the Civil Rights Act of 1964 became law. The Civil Rights Act made it illegal to discriminate against any American because of their race, gender, skin color, religion, or where they were born.

The next year, the Voting Rights Act of 1965 was passed. It protected the right African-Americans had to vote in government elections. Progress was finally being made.

Johnson's signing of the Civil Rights Act was broadcast live on television and radio.

A tragic event happened on the morning of April 4, 1968. Martin Luther King Jr. was shot and killed while he was on a hotel balcony in Memphis, Tennessee. The man who shot him was James Earl Ray. Ray was an escaped prisoner who had been on the run since 1967.

After reports of King's death spread across the nation, angry citizens took to the streets. In many major cities, riots broke out. The National Guard and the army were called in to try to control the situation.

King had spent his life fighting for equal rights for African-Americans. His words still inspire people today.

Mourners walk through the streets of King's hometown of Atlanta, Georgia, after his death.

New laws

Several new laws were passed because of the Civil Rights Movement. Three of the most important ones helped make the United States a more equal place in which to live and work.

Civil Rights Act, 1964

Employers are not allowed to discriminate against people based on their "color, religion, or national origin." This act also makes segregation illegal in all public places.

Voting Rights Act, 1965

Some states had set up tests that people had to pass in order to be allowed to vote. This act makes those tests illegal.

Fair Housing Act, 1968

African-Americans who wanted to buy or rent a place to live were often discriminated against. This act makes that practice illegal.

Famous civil rights march from Selma to Montgomery in 1965

Chapter 5
The fight goes on

The African-American community has come a long way in the fight for equality, but things are far from perfect. For example, African-Americans have a higher rate of graduating college in 2017 than ever before, but it is still not as high as the rate for white students.

Also, the average income for an African-American family is better than what it was in 1963. However, it is still only about two-thirds of the average income for all families in the United States.

Fewer African-American families live in poverty today than in the 1960s. Clearly things are getting better—but there's still a lot of work to be done.

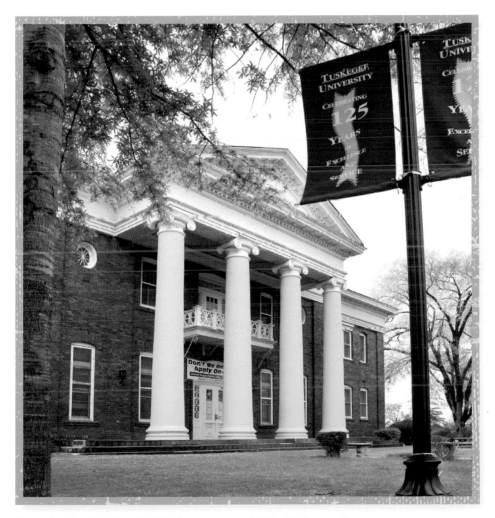

Founded by Booker T. Washington in 1881, Tuskegee Institute celebrated its 125th anniversary in 2006.

Alex Haley, author of *Roots*, speaking to the attendees at the Santa Barbara Writers Conference.

The 1950s and 1960s were the most dramatic years for the Civil Rights Movement. However, there were notable achievements in the 1970s and 1980s as well.

In 1976 the book *Roots* was published. It is about a man who was brought from Africa to America as a slave. The story then follows his relatives through American history. Both the book and TV miniseries were very successful.

They exposed many people to the reality of slavery for the first time.

Since 1976, the United States has celebrated Black History Month during February. In 1983, President Ronald Reagan made Martin Luther King Jr. Day a national holiday. It is now held every January, on the third Monday of the month.

President Reagan signing the Martin Luther King Jr. Day Bill.

The fight for civil rights continued into the 2000s. With modern ways of communicating, such as the Internet and texting, it is easier than ever for activists to "get the word out." All a person has to do is post something online.

One big example of online activism is the Black Lives Matter movement. It began in 2012 on Twitter as the hashtag #BlackLivesMatter.

People were angry about recent events in which they felt black people had been horribly, unfairly, and wrongly treated. They posted their thoughts and opinions online to demand change.

People also took part in marches and protests, telling everyone how important equality is. These marches and protests happened not just in the United States, but in other countries, too.

Black Lives Matter marches and protests took place all around the world.

The Civil Rights Movement inspired some of today's most amazing people.

Oprah Winfrey

At a time when there were very few good job opportunities for African-Americans, especially women, Oprah Winfrey decided on a media career. Today she runs a media empire and is believed to be the wealthiest African-American in the world.

Colin Powell was born to an immigrant family in Harlem, New York, in 1937. He went on to become the first African-American Secretary of State in 2001.

Colin Powell

Barack Obama with his wife and daughters at the White House.

Barack Obama worked hard, attended Harvard University, and taught and practiced civil rights law. In 2008, he was elected the first African-American President of the United States.

The fight for civil rights has been long. It has not been easy. But there are many reasons to be hopeful that one day all people will be treated equally.

How to be an activist

Being an activist means speaking out about what you believe is right. Which causes are important to you? Here are some ways to get involved.

Students in New York marching for peace.

Look for activist groups in your town. See if there is some way you can help them. They might need help with making signs or handing out fliers.

Does your school have an activism club? If so, join in! If not, you could talk to a teacher about starting one.

Write a letter to your local newspaper, or post your thoughts on a safe website. Use your words to tell people what you believe.

Most important of all—don't do nothing! If you see or know of someone being treated unfairly, don't keep it a secret. Tell your parents, your teachers, or a trusted adult.

Kids holding signs during a protest in Pennsylvania.

Quiz

Can you answer these questions about civil rights?

1 From where were people taken and brought to America as slaves?

2 What was the name given to people who wanted to stop slavery?

3 What law was passed in 1865 to abolish slavery in the United States?

4 What common phrase was used to refer to segregation?

5 What was Rosa Parks arrested for refusing to do?

6 What type of protest did people hold to stop segregation at department stores?

7 Which civil rights leader promoted using violence if necessary?

8 Who gave the "I have a dream" speech at the March on Washington?

9 In which year was the Civil Rights Act passed?

10 In which month is Black History Month celebrated?

11 Which president made Martin Luther King Jr. Day a national holiday?

12 Who was the first African-American President of the United States?

Answers on page 63

Glossary

abolitionist
person who wanted to stop, or abolish, slavery

activist
person who takes action or speaks out about something they believe is right or wrong

boycott
when people stop using a business or service to show they don't agree with how it is behaving

civil rights
laws that make sure people are treated fairly

civil war
war between two groups of people in one country

discriminate
to treat someone unfairly because of their characteristics or beliefs

election
event where people choose their government leaders by voting

equality
when people have the same rights and are treated in the same way

government
group of people who make a country's laws

historic
important event in history

lawsuit
disagreement between two people or groups
that is dealt with in a court

plantation
large farm often used to grow sugarcane or cotton

protest
event where a group of people gather to show
they disagree with something

racism
discriminating against someone because of their
skin color

segregation
act of keeping black and white people apart

sit-in
event where people protest by sitting somewhere

Supreme Court
top court in the United States. The Supreme
Court decides the country's most important cases

Index

abolitionists 8–9, 10

activism 25, 52, 56–57

Africa 6, 50

Black History Month
51

Black Lives Matter
52–53

books 9, 50

boycotts 22–23, 28, 33

Bridges, Ruby 24–25

Civil Rights Act
42–43, 46

Civil War 10–11

colleges 9, 27, 48, 49

Douglass, Frederick
8–9

Eckford, Elizabeth 19

Eisenhower, Dwight D.
18

Fair Housing Act 47

farming 7, 10

Jim Crow laws 14

Johnson, Lyndon B.
38–39, 42, 43

Kennedy, John F.
38–39, 40–41, 42

King Jr., Martin Luther
26–27, 28, 32–33, 34,
36–37, 44–45, 51

Lincoln, Abraham
10–11

Little Rock 18–19

Malcom X 30–31, 33

March on Washington
34–35, 36

marches 33, 34–35, 36,
46–47, 56

Montgomery 21,
22–23, 27, 28

NAACP 17, 18

Obama, Barack 55

Parks, Rosa 20–21,
22–23, 28

plantations 6, 7

Plessy, Homer 16–17

Powell, Colin 54

protests 19, 33,
  34, 53, 57

Reagan, Ronald 51

schools 5, 15, 18–19,
  24–25, 57

segregation 12, 13,
  14–15, 17, 23, 29

"separate but equal"
  14–15, 17, 18

sit-ins 28, 29, 33

slavery 6–7, 8, 9, 10,
  50–51

Supreme Court
  16–17, 18

Tubman, Harriet 8

Tuskegee Institute
  9, 49

Underground Railroad
  8

Voting Rights Act
  43, 47

Washington, Booker T.
  9, 49

Washington, DC
  34–35

Winfrey, Oprah 54

Answers to the Quiz:

1. Africa; **2.** Abolitionist; **3.** 13th Amendment; **4.** "Separate but equal"; **5.** For refusing to give up her bus seat to a white passenger; **6.** Sit-in; **7.** Malcolm X; **8.** Martin Luther King Jr.; **9.** 1964; **10.** February; **11.** Ronald Reagan; **12.** Barack Obama

A LEVEL FOR EVERY READER

This book is a part of an exciting four-level reading series to support children in developing the habit of reading widely for both pleasure and information. Each book is designed to develop a child's reading skills, fluency, grammar awareness, and comprehension in order to build confidence and enjoyment when reading.

Ready for a Level 3 (Beginning to Read Alone) book

A child should:

- be able to read many words without needing to stop and break them down into sound parts.
- read smoothly, in phrases and with expression, and at a good pace.
- self-correct when a word or sentence doesn't sound right or doesn't make sense.

A valuable and shared reading experience

For many children, reading requires much effort but adult participation can make reading both fun and easier. Here are a few tips on how to use this book with a young reader:

Check out the contents together:

- read about the book on the back cover and talk about the contents page to help heighten interest and expectation.
- ask the reader to make predictions about what they think will happen next.
- talk about the information he/she might want to find out.

Encourage fluent reading:

- encourage reading aloud in fluent, expressive phrases, making full use of punctuation and thinking about the meaning; if helpful, choose a sentence to read aloud to help demonstrate reading with expression.

Praise, share, and talk:

- notice if the reader is responding to the text by self-correcting and varying his/her voice.
- encourage the reader to recall specific details after each chapter.
- let him/her pick out interesting words and discuss what they mean.
- talk about what he/she found most interesting or important and show your own enthusiasm for the book.
- read the quiz at the end of the book and encourage the reader to answer the questions, if necessary, by turning back to the relevant pages to find the answers.

Series consultant, Dr. Linda Gambrell, Distinguished Professor of Education at Clemson University, has served as President of the National Reading Conference, the College Reading Association, and the International Reading Association.